zendoodle coloring

Cozy Comfort

Cozy Comfort

The Warmth of Home to Color and Display

illustrations by
Deborah Muller

CASTLE POINT BOOKS
NEW YORK

ZENDOODLE COLORING: COZY COMFORT.
Copyright © 2023 by St. Martin's Press. All rights reserved.
Printed in Canada. For information, address
St. Martin's Publishing Group, 120 Broadway, New York, NY 10271.

www.castlepointbooks.com

The Castle Point Books trademark is owned by Castle Point Publishing, LLC.
Castle Point books are published and distributed by St. Martin's Publishing Group.

ISBN 978-1-250-28550-8 (trade paperback)

Our books may be purchased in bulk for promotional, educational, or business use.
Please contact your local bookseller or the Macmillan Corporate and Premium
Sales Department at 1-800-221-7945, extension 5442, or by email
at MacmillanSpecialMarkets@macmillan.com.

First Edition: 2023

10 9 8 7 6 5 4 3 2 1

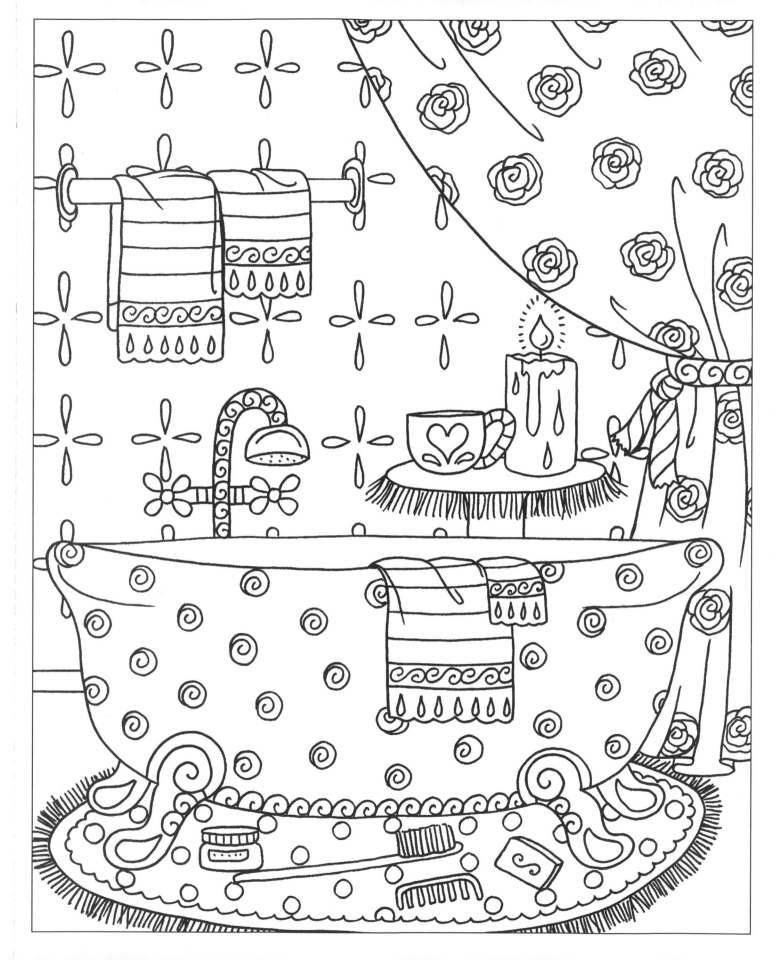

TEA